THE YOUNGER
GENTLEMAN'S
GUIDE

To: Evan
To the Gentleman
Son-in-law
I am so proud of
all the time!
Maybe one nugget

TOM McWHORTER

will bless
you!

The Younger Gentleman's Guide

Copyright © 2024 Tom McWhorter

Published by Book Ripple Publishing
www.BookRipple.com

All rights reserved. No part of this book may be reproduced or transmitted in any form or by any means, electronic or mechanical, including photocopying and recording, or by an information storage and retrieval system, without permission in writing from the author.

ISBN: 978-1-951797-66-9

Printed in the United States of America

To order go to:
www.tommcwhorter.com

INTRODUCTION

Almost every week, I either observe or hear about some young man who seems ignorant about any sort of decorum.

In today's world full of "gentlemen's" clubs and absentee fathers, more and more boys are growing up with no example or, even worse, a bad example of what being a man is all about. Even the dictionary in the spell-check section of my word-processing software contains the word "manner" but not "manners."

My desire is that this manual may help all boys on the brink of manhood, as well as their parents. Many recognize a gentleman when they see one but can't quite put their finger on what that means.

In this current day, even the terms "lady" or "ma'am" or "gentleman" could offend some. They may feel they are being either excluded or boxed in by ideas connoted by those words. Maybe they're right. Maybe we don't need a label for respectful behavior. Perhaps the best we should hope is that others might say of us, "I like the way he treats people."

Wouldn't any man want that said of him? I suspect that would be true for you. Otherwise, you probably wouldn't even be holding this book.

I just prefer the time-honored term "gentleman." Admittedly, the term needs some explaining, and that's what this guide is about. Hopefully, its suggestions will foster better behavior than that which some men have practiced.

Regretfully, this objectionable behavior has all too often given a deservedly bad name to masculinity. I believe that good manners are a way to honor others and respect yourself as a man.

Can many of the points in this guide apply to women and girls as well? Certainly. I'll leave that book for a woman to write. This one is man-to-man.

The purpose of good manners is not simply rule following, but putting others at ease and making them feel comfortable.

What is acceptable in one culture, however, is sometimes unacceptable and offensive in another.

For example, people in the United States think nothing of eating with the left hand. But in many countries around the world, eating with the left hand is considered repulsive and should be avoided, regardless of which is

the dominant hand. More subtle differences exist even within the U.S.

As you read this book, please keep in mind not only the culture of your current experience but also the culture with which you desire to be aligned, whatever that may be. I have written this guide from the perspective of the culture within which I live.

I neither pretend to be any sort of final authority, nor do I always follow what I have written. Like everyone else on this planet, I am a flawed human being and make mistakes. As a Christian, I am, as the bumper sticker says, "not perfect, just forgiven."

A word about dating: Call me a prude, but having learned firsthand the hard way, I've experienced the permanent damage dating can do to both parties.

My recommendation is to hang out at group activities until you are ready to think about marriage.

In this book, I have outlined what I believe to be the dating behavior that should begin before marriage and continue thereafter with your wife, regardless of when you decide to begin dating.

Through listening to and watching my father, and by practicing on my delighted mother, I learned what I now understand to be the elements of being a gentleman.

When I saw my own 13-year-old son beginning the process of manhood, I wanted to convey in writing for him, to the extent possible, what my father taught me and what I have since learned by observation and reading.

Contents

Introduction	3
CHAPTER ONE: Personal Hygiene	11
CHAPTER TWO: General Manners	15
CHAPTER THREE: At the Table	31
CHAPTER FOUR: Dating	39
CHAPTER FIVE: Church	45
CHAPTER SIX: Travel	47
CHAPTER SEVEN: Clothing	53
Conclusion	61

THE YOUNGER GENTLEMAN'S GUIDE

Chapter One

Personal Hygiene

Make your bed every morning.

Shower daily using soap.

Put on deodorant after you get out of the shower.

Brush or comb your hair after showering while your hair is still damp. It's easier that way.

Brush your teeth after breakfast, before leaving home.

Keep your fingernails and toenails clean and trimmed.

If you grow your beard, keep it neatly trimmed. Otherwise, shave daily.

When away from home, always go to the men's room to adjust your clothes or attend to any matters of personal hygiene or appearance.

In public bathrooms, conversation with strangers is probably not a good idea. Take care of business and get out as quickly as possible. Use a paper towel or fresh tissue to clean up any mess you make.

On leaving, use a paper towel to open the door, then toss it in the closest trash can you find.

Whenever possible, leave at least one urinal between you and the next man.

If you cannot wait to go to the men's room to remove some small amount of matter from your eye, nose, etc., use the handkerchief you carry in your pocket.

Do not look at your handkerchief before refolding it. You've seen the stuff before, and you know what it looks like. Don't call attention to it.

When you feel a sneeze or cough coming on, pull out your handkerchief and cover your mouth and nose.

If you forgot your hankie, or can't get it out soon enough, sneeze into the crook of your arm.

If you must pick your teeth, do so when not in the presence of others.

If you must spit, go to the men's room.

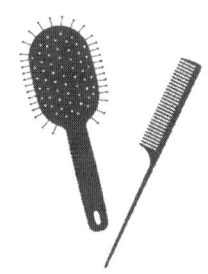

Long hair is okay, but don't let it cover your eyes. People want to see all of your face.

If you need to have your hair cut before an important occasion, do it at least a week in advance so you don't look like a newly shorn lamb.

Have a primary care physician. If you have a medical need, have your doctor attend to it. Don't complain about it.

Visit the dentist every six months.

Chapter Two

General Manners

Read the book of Proverbs in the Bible.

Read George Washington's brief *Rules of Civility.*

If you ask anyone for anything, say, "Please."

If someone gives you something or does something for you, say, "Thank you."

Don't point at others.

Remove your hat when going indoors. Although you may love the message your hat conveys, you don't need it to protect you from the sun in there.

When a guest enters your home, stand, turn off the TV if it is on, shake their hand, take their coat, and offer them a chair and a drink, even if it is only water.

If you were eating, follow the table manners section (Chapter Three) on what to do when an additional guest arrives at your table.

When you arrange an appointment with someone, exchange contact information in case either of you has a last-minute change of plans.

When the appointed time arrives, be on time. This shows respect for the other person.

If you know that you are going to be more than

15 minutes late for any meeting or appointment, call, apologize, and say what time you think you can be there.

Return phone calls, voice mails, and texts within 24 hours.

Pay attention to a person's character, not their appearance.

Don't cut in line.

Treat your family members with respect.

Remember that your character is demonstrated by what you do when you think no one will find out.

Treat the elderly with respect.

When someone gives you a gift and is not present for you to thank, mail a thank-you note within two or three days.

This lets them know you received it.

If the gift was cash, never mention the amount, but say how you might spend it.

If you borrow something from someone, establish a time and place at which you will return it. If you need additional time, ask. Often the lender will give you permission.

Keep your hands away from your ears, nose, and mouth.

Knock and ask permission before entering someone's room.

Close doors carefully. Don't slam them.

If you must put your feet on a piece of furniture, make sure it is a stool or an ottoman.

Obey your parents and accept discipline from them. You will need to know how to do this with other authority figures later in life.

Obey laws.

Knuckle popping communicates to others that, for some reason, you are uneasy in their presence. Don't do it.

Don't bite your nails or chew the inside of your mouth. Both are unhealthy.

Place litter in trash receptacles.

When someone is speaking at a podium or performing onstage, make no noise or light using anything you may have with you, such as paper or electronic devices.

When you are waiting on a response from someone who is helping you, supervising you, or talking with you, you want to convey patience.

Be still. Fidgeting conveys impatience.

Offer your arm to the elderly when walking up and down curbs and stairs.

When going through doors, look behind you. Hold the door for the next person.

When someone drops something, pick it up for them.

If someone falls, help them up.

Leave spaces in a better state of cleanliness than you found them.

If you made or helped make any mess, clean it up. You might even help clean up messes you didn't make.

Always carry at least $5 in ones, and a larger bill or two if you can afford it.

When meeting another man, look him straight

in the eye, smile, and extend your hand to give a firm handshake, but don't try to break his hand.

LISTEN for and remember his name.

For more tips on handshakes, there are plenty of videos online (keywords: how men shake hands).

When meeting a woman, look her straight in the eye, smile, and make sure your right hand is at your side, not in your pocket.

By seeing your hand there, she can see that you welcome a handshake. It is her choice to extend her hand if she wishes a handshake.

If a woman initiates a hug, you may make her feel comfortable by accepting it, but shoulder-level contact only – no waists.

If you are wearing a hat when introduced to a woman, remove it with your left hand if you are in a shaded area.

If you are not, lift the bill or rim slightly with your left hand, then put it back down.

Using the left hand for this hat tip leaves your right hand free for a handshake if she initiates it.

When introduced to someone, respond with, "Nice to meet you" or "Hi, how are you?"

Be sure to LISTEN for and remember their name.

When introducing yourself to someone, give your name first:

"Hi, my name is Tom."

When introducing two people, name the woman or the older person first:

> "Helen, I'd like you to meet George."

> "Mrs. Jones, I'd like you to meet my friend, Bob."

If you feel the need to cock your chin when being introduced, cock it down, not up.

If you can think of a sincere compliment, give it.

When complimenting a woman, the most appropriate occasion for complimenting her appearance is on a date.

Also, be sure it is accompanied by other compliments not related to appearance.

Stand when an adult or a woman enters the room. Offer your seat if there are no more.

If there are more chairs than people, go find more chairs.

When you're seated in a standing-room-only situation, offer your seat to the closest elderly, pregnant, or disabled person, or woman over the age of 12.

In today's world of gender consciousness, if you have the slightest doubt about someone's gender, say, "Yes, please" or "No, thank you."

If you must whisper to someone, do it when not in the presence of others so they don't feel left out of the conversation.

Unless reporting a crime or missing person, avoid using someone's race to describe them.

If you must make a comment on someone's physical appearance, make it complimentary.

Make your speech uplifting, rather than condescending.

When someone else makes a negative comment, either change the subject or say nothing. Sometimes, that's the best thing to do.

Not everything that can be corrected should be corrected.

When you hear a negative comment about someone who's not present, defend them.

Always say, "Excuse me" or "Pardon me" if you bump into someone.

Remember that when you are trying to make an impression, the impression you are

going to make is that you are trying to make an impression.

Not surprisingly to the people of the Victorian era, Benjamin Disraeli won the election to the post of Prime Minister.

His opponent, William Gladstone, was a very clever and witty person. Based on his wit and experience, he had what it took to win the election.

What made the difference, however, was summed up by Winston Churchill's mother after having dinner with both Disraeli and Gladstone a week before the election.

She explained, "When I left the dining room after sitting next to Gladstone, I thought he was the cleverest man in England. But when I sat next to Disraeli, I left feeling that I was the cleverest woman."

Spend conversational time listening, rather than thinking of what you will say next.

Being gross doesn't make you look cool.

Much of being a good conversationalist is being a good listener.

When tempted to use profanity in communicating with others, depend on your character, education, and vocabulary to deliver your message.

Learn to converse intelligently with adults by asking questions about things that might interest them.

Maintain eye contact during conversation.

If you're wondering whether you should tell a questionable story, not telling is the better choice.

Always tell the unstretched truth. Telling false stories as true just to see if someone will believe you is inappropriate unless it is clear you are joking.

Think before you speak.

Consider your audience.

When someone compliments you, respond with a simple, "Thank you."

Don't make excuses or apologize. Accept the compliment as intended.

When you've encountered misfortune and someone says, "I'm sorry," they are not claiming responsibility, but offering consolation.

The appropriate response is, "Thank you."

When you cannot avoid walking between two

people in conversation, quietly say, "Excuse me" or "Pardon me."

The same is true when you must walk in front of someone in a store who is looking at merchandise on the shelf.

When you feel isolated in a room full of people, find someone else who appears to feel the same way. Smile! That's your person to make friends with.

When someone asks, "How are you doing?" it is usually a greeting, not a question.

The proper response is, "Great," or "Fine."

Unless it's a close friend, they probably don't want the results of your latest physical exam or a recounting of your most recent illness.

Never objectify women, even if none are present.

THE YOUNGER GENTLEMAN'S GUIDE

Chapter Three

At the Table

Wait until your host/hostess is seated before sitting.

If a hostess places a woman on your right, pull her chair out from the table, then push it in as she sits. If there are other women in close proximity, help them as well, if necessary.

If you have a woman with you, seat her on your right. It is the place of honor. Help her with her chair.

Introduce yourself to those around you.

Eat only after the host/hostess has begun eating, and after those within comfortable speaking distance have been served. This applies for every course.

Eat and drink what is placed before you. If you or your date have specific allergies, let the server know.

Don't ask for anything not presented unless it is water. Then say, "May I please have some water?" If you don't want to eat something, make no comment. Just leave it there.

Stand whenever a latecomer comes to the table. If there is not a chair already there for them, find one.

When any unexpected visitor arrives, stop eating and drinking, stand, and ask them to join you.

In a restaurant, if you happen to see someone you know, make your greeting brief, then find your own table unless they insist you join them.

Do not take longer to order or eat than those in a superior position to you (the host/hostess, teacher, supervisor, older person, or one who is paying).

If your host/hostess makes no suggestions from the menu, ask what they'd recommend.

Never complain about the food or service, regardless of who is paying.

In restaurants, remember your server's name if they give it. If they don't, address them as "Server," "Waiter," or "Waitress."

If you call them, "Sir" or "Ma'am," you may disturb diners at other tables – they may think you are addressing them!

Also, using a server's name is more considerate. If the server doesn't give their name, ask for it.

When you are paying, don't take the server to task over small errors.

Make conversation the focus of the meal, rather than food consumption.

If the group wants to split a large check evenly and your meal was smaller than the rest, accept the division and keep that in mind the next time the group gets together.

Follow your host/hostess's lead on everything, especially on ordering dessert.

Ask for a to-go box only if you are paying, and not in an upscale restaurant.

As soon as you're seated, place your

THE YOUNGER GENTLEMAN'S GUIDE

napkin on your lap and your silverware on either side of your plate, if it was not already.

Do so in this manner:

- the fork goes to the left of the plate,
- the knife to the right with the blade toward the plate, and
- the spoon to the right of the knife.

If food is too hot to eat, don't blow on it. Wait for it to cool or, if you've taken a bite that's too hot, take a sip of water to cool it off.

Place used silverware on your plate, not back on the tablecloth.

Wipe your mouth with your napkin before drinking from your glass.

The best time to use the men's room and wash

your hands is immediately after orders are placed.

Keep your mouth closed while chewing.

Wait until you have swallowed what is in your mouth before taking another bite.

Never talk with food in your mouth.

Take bites small enough so that you can finish a bite in a reasonable amount of time to answer someone's question.

Don't sing or hum at the table.

Keep all four legs of your chair on the floor.

Don't play with silverware, napkins, food, etc.

If you must belch, cover your mouth, turn slightly away from the nearest person, and let the air out quietly. If it is heard, say, "Excuse me."

Sit with your hips back in your chair, lean forward, and raise your arm off the table with each bite.

Don't lean over your plate or bowl.

If you are right-handed, keep your left hand in your lap unless you are cutting or otherwise preparing food. Vice versa for left-handed people.

Your hat is acceptable at the table only when eating in full sun outdoors.

Don't leave a restaurant with a toothpick hanging from your lips.

Keep your elbows off the table.

THE YOUNGER GENTLEMAN'S GUIDE

Chapter Four

Dating

Before starting a dating relationship, remember that you pay for everything. However, if your date offers to pay for something, graciously accept.

When asking a friend for a date, don't ask, "What are your plans for Saturday?" or "Are you doing anything Saturday night?"

Say, for example, "There is a party at Taylor's house on Saturday night at 7:00. It should be over about 11:00. Would you like to go with me?"

Be sure to tell her the attire for the event. She wants to know. If you're unsure, tell her what you'll be wearing. Remember, your job is to make her look good.

Walk your date to and from your car.

Be prepared with an umbrella, and be sure your date gets most, or all, of the coverage.

If you are unsure whether your date's parents already know, tell them where you are going, what time you plan to return, and ask if that is acceptable.

Treat your date's family members and pets with respect. Also, a few clean jokes appropriate for different age levels never hurt.

Know how to play with children in an appropriate way.

Allow friendship with her parents to develop naturally. Don't try to force it.

Open the car door for your date. Wait to see that she and all her clothing are completely inside the car before closing the door.

Insist that passengers wear seat belts. They'll be protected and you won't get a ticket.

If you take a girl out more than once, have friends join you by the third outing. If you like her that much, she should meet your friends. She'll feel honored as well.

Remember that having a date is about showing her how awesome you think she is. It's not about you.

When introducing your date to others, mention her name first.

> "Emma, I'd like you to meet Jackson."

When introducing her to an adult, mention the adult's name first.

If you go to an event where you are the only one your date knows, introduce her to a female friend, if there is one at the function. This will make her feel more comfortable.

If you go to a dance, dance!

When taking seats in the middle of an already occupied row in a theater or stadium, let your date follow you in.

You should be first in saying, "Excuse me" and in causing those already seated to allow you to pass.

Pass others facing them.

Help your date with her chair at the dinner table any time she has to get up during the meal.

When ordering from a menu, say something like, "The chicken looks good!" to give your date an idea of your price range, but be prepared to pay joyfully for the most expensive item on the menu.

Better yet, choose a restaurant where you'll be comfortable paying for the most expensive choice on the menu. Then you won't have to hint.

Do not discuss the prices of items on the menu or the amount of the bill. If you must dispute the bill, excuse yourself from the table and discuss it with your server.

Leave a tip for good service (15%–20%).

Open doors for women.

Help women with their coats.

Make sure your date walks on the handrail side of the stairs and on the side of the sidewalk away from the street.

Have your date home by the time you told her parents you would.

If you enjoyed your date's company, tell her.

When you ask to see your date again, be specific about when and where.

If you tell someone you will call, do it. If you don't plan on calling, don't say you will.

Thank her for her time, even if you have no plans to call again. If you are sure you'll never take her on another date, don't "ghost" her; that is totally ignoring her. Ask if you can just be friends.

Chapter Five

Church

Once the music starts, find a seat quickly, sit down, and pay attention to what is going on up front.

Introduce yourself to those sitting around you.

Avoid turning around during the service.

When you are sitting at the end of a pew and others want to share your pew, move down. Don't make them crawl over you.

Leave with anything you brought.

Smile. God really does love you!

THE YOUNGER GENTLEMAN'S GUIDE

Chapter Six

Travel

As a driver:

> Attend to basic auto maintenance (wiper blades, oil, coolant, tire pressure) to prevent unplanned stops and delays.
>
> The driver chooses the music.
>
> If you're driving, ask the shotgun passenger their preference.
>
> Be familiar with the route before getting in the car. You'll be able to pay better attention to passengers as you won't have to be interrupted or distracted by digital navigational aids.

Speed limits are often established by residents of the area through which you are traveling. Be respectful of those limits and residents. You're not on the track at Indy.

Be mindful of passengers' seating preferences which are often based on height, size, age, or the nature of the group's relationships.

As a passenger:

>Always choose the least desirable seat, usually the rear middle.

>Defer to women, the disabled, and elderly.

>When the driver makes a rest/gas stop, use the men's room whether you need to or not. That way, the

driver won't have to make a special stop later to accommodate you.

While the driver is filling up with gas, clean the windshield and rear window.

Whenever you leave the car, take your litter out and dispose of it.

If the trip is over, take all your personal belongings with you.

Generally:

Learn to change a tire and jump-start a car.

For needs beyond your expertise, know what number to call for emergency roadside service.

Take stationery with you on an overnight trip so

that during the return trip you can write thank-you notes to those who have hosted you for dinner or provided you overnight lodging. That way, you will have them ready to mail when you return home.

When you are an overnight guest in someone's home, take them out to dinner.

Allow others to exit an elevator, or any other conveyance, before trying to enter.

Check the weather before you leave, and pack appropriately.

Plan your packing list beginning with your head.

Move from hats to coats and ties to

shirts to underwear to slacks to socks and shoes to toiletries.

The Younger Gentleman's Guide

Chapter Seven

Clothing

For Business Professional attire or more formal settings, wear a suit, leather dress shoes, socks the same color as or darker than your suit, a white shirt, and a contrasting tie that complements your suit.

Straight collar shirts with stays are better than button downs for business professional.

Button downs can look crumpled by the end of a day or evening.

If an event calls for Business Casual, a creased pair of slacks, a long-sleeve sport shirt, and shoes to complement your slacks should suffice.

If the weather is warm, short sleeves are acceptable.

When wearing a suit or blazer, wear a long-sleeve dress shirt. Never wear a short-sleeve shirt with a dress jacket.

If you can afford it, own a good pair of both black shoes and brown shoes.

Have your suit coats and blazers tailored so that about 1/4 inch of cuff shows below your jacket sleeves.

Keep your suit coat buttoned when standing or walking. Unbutton it to sit down.

If the plackets on the long sleeves of your dress shirt have buttons, button them before putting on your shirt. It's easier.

Learn to iron your dress shirts or to touch them up after they've been only gently worn. There are plenty of videos online (keywords: men ironing dress shirts).

Keep the right-hand edge of the front placket of your dress shirt lined up with the edge of your belt buckle and the fly on your slacks. The line formed is called the gig line.
Spit-shine leather shoes about once every six weeks, and brush them every day.

Use a shoe horn to put them on.

I recommend wearing rubber gloves when shining your shoes, so as not to get polish on your hands, as it can take days to wear off. You'll want clean hands and fingernails, especially if you're wearing a suit or tux.

Learn how to spit-shine your shoes. There are plenty of videos online (keywords: spit shining shoes).

Generally, any occasion that is casual enough

for short sleeves is casual enough for a knit (polo) shirt rather than one that needs starch/ironing.

If the event is very casual, such as an outdoor summer barbecue, shorts with sandals or clean sneakers are also acceptable.

Carry a pocket comb, a handkerchief, some small writing paper, and a pen or pencil.

You may even consider carrying two handkerchiefs so you have a clean spare for another person's benefit.

Robert de Niro's character in *The Intern* explains it well. Watch him explain it (keywords: The Intern, Robert de Niro, handkerchief).

Learn to tie a bow tie. There are plenty of videos online (keywords: tying a bow tie).

Tie your necktie so that the larger end covers the smaller.

After tying your tie, pass the small end through the loop on the back of the larger.

Learn to tie a four-in-hand, half Windsor, and full Windsor. There are plenty of videos online.

Ties come in different lengths and thicknesses. Experience will teach you when to use each knot.

Your tie should touch or barely cover your belt buckle.

If you can afford it, have two pairs of jeans: One with holes and smudges for wearing around the house, and another without blemish for wearing with a nice shirt to parties.

I bought one of my favorite pairs for $7 at

the Salvation Army. They came complete with holes!

If you have room, store soft knit shirts in a drawer rather than on hangers in the closet, so that they don't have "hanger mountains" that stick up off your shoulders when you put them on.

If you must store them hanging, use a sturdy hanger (rather than a wire or thin hanger) to help the shirts keep their shape.

Formal or Black Tie attire calls for a black tuxedo including a cummerbund, a white formal shirt with studs (removable buttons) and cuff links, a self-tied (not pre-tied) bow tie, and black formal shoes.

Black and white attire is the classic standard. It is classic because it exhibits your desire that your female companion be the one who stands out.

Remember, it's your job to make sure she does.

Feel free to develop your own style. Just don't make it the most memorable thing about you.

THE YOUNGER GENTLEMAN'S GUIDE

Conclusion

While there is nothing particularly Southern about being a gentleman, I often heard others describe my father, during his life and particularly after his death, as a "true Southern gentleman."

As I have come to understand gentlemanly behavior, indeed he was. This book is dedicated to his memory.

DISCLAIMER: I do not address online behavior, although my suggestions about respectful communication with others apply there as well. One guideline I do feel is worth adding, however, is getting a person's permission before disseminating their likeness.

Notes to Self

NOTES TO SELF

Congratulations!

When others describe you, they will call you a *gentleman*, and that is a badge of honor.